DAN CRAWFORD

HEROES OF THE CROSS

DAVID BRAINERD

WILLIAM CAREY

JAMES CHALMERS

DAN CRAWFORD

WILFRED GRENFELL

DAVID LIVINGSTONE

MARY SLESSOR

JOHN WESLEY

DAN CRAWFORD

MARSHALLS

Marshall Morgan & Scott
1 Bath Street, London EC1V 9LB

Copyright © Marshall Morgan & Scott 1982

First published by Oliphants Ltd 1956
First issued in paperback in Lakeland 1963

This edition in Marshalls 1982
Impression number 10 9 8 7 6 5 4 3 2 1

ISBN: 0 551 00953 5

Printed in Great Britain by Richard Clay (The Chaucer Press) Ltd,
Bungay, Suffolk

CONTENTS

DAN CRAWFORD'S BOYHOOD

OFF the west coast of Scotland, close to where the River Clyde reaches the sea, are to be found many lovely islands. All are famed for their great beauty and are, in consequence, favourite holiday resorts. Perhaps some of you who are reading this book have, at some time or other, spent a holiday in Bute or Arran.

According to legend, it was on the Isle of Arran that Robert Bruce watched the spider which encouraged him to go on with the fight for the freedom of his people; and from this island he returned to the mainland to lead his followers to victory.

The hero of this book, Dan Crawford, was descended from folk who had lived on the island for centuries. His father and grandfather sailed their own small coasting vessel between Arran and the Scottish mainland. From the island they carried cargoes of sandstone and to it they came back with loads of coal.

Dan's father, Archibald Crawford, decided, however, to set up his home on the mainland at a town called Gourock, and here Dan was born on December 7th, 1870. The little lad was barely four years old when his father died, leaving

Mrs. Crawford with two young children to bring up. She kept a small sweet shop, where she had to work hard to make ends meet.

Living so near to the sea, Dan loved nothing better than to sail in the bay. Sometimes his adventures alarmed his mother, for he used to go in a friend's yacht in all kinds of weather. In the end she made him promise not to go out again, but one day the temptation proved too strong; Dan went out with his friend, expecting to get home before he was missed. Unfortunately for them, the wind dropped and the boat was becalmed. The lads had no oars and had to stay where they were for hours; until, in fact, a breeze sprang up which carried them back. He reached home in the early hours of the morning to find his mother sitting up waiting anxiously. She did not need to scold him. The look of distress on her face was enough to stop him from breaking his promise again.

Dan left school at a much younger age than that at which boys and girls leave today and began to earn a living. The wage was small, but it helped his mother and sister in the struggle to make ends meet. After a short time in a solicitor's office, he took a post as a book-keeper. All that he earned was cheerfully handed over to his mother.

One Sunday evening, he visited a mission hall where he heard a simple explanation of God's way of salvation through the Lord Jesus Christ. Before he went home, he knew the peace which comes to those who yield their lives to Christ. So great was his joy that from then on he sang gaily on his way to work and called out cheery greetings to everyone he met, whether he knew them or not! He also wanted to share his new found joy with others. At lunch time he used to hurry down to the docks, keeping a sharp look-out for anyone who looked to need a good square meal. There were many such in those days, when men who could not get work received no help with which to buy food. With such a one Dan would share his sandwiches and to him would speak of the loving God who feeds the birds of the air and looks after all who put their trust in Him.

In the evenings he would go into the streets, speaking to any who would listen about his Saviour. The word "Gospel" means "good news" and we all like being able to spread good news. This urge to share his joy with others was to affect his whole life. One day he read in his Bible, "Go ye into all the world and preach the Gospel to every creature" (*Mark* 16:15). God was calling him to leave home and friends in order to share the Good News with people who had never heard the name of Jesus.

II

THE CALL TO AFRICA

WHEN he was seventeen Dan visited Keswick in the Lake District. In this town, surrounded by mountains and lakes of great beauty, Christian people meet every year to worship God and to learn how they can live the kind of lives which He wants His people to live. With him went several Christian friends from Greenock, among them John Colville, who later became a Member of Parliament and started prayer-meetings in the House of Commons. These two, John Colville and Dan Crawford, had often witnessed together for Christ in the streets of Greenock. They did so also in Keswick. Among those who heard them speak in the market square was a young man named Greenwood. He was deeply impressed by their message and from that night became a follower of Christ and a leader of Christian work in the town.

Twenty-four years later Dan Crawford came to Keswick again. He was then a famous missionary who had been invited to speak to the thousands of Christians gathered there. The meeting took place in a huge tent and Dan had to go straight from the service to the station to catch a train to London, where the Prime

Minister wanted to see him about matters concerning the part of Africa where Dan had made his home. He was driven to the station in a car, the driver of which proudly told him that his name was Daniel Crawford Greenwood. He was the son of the young man who had been converted when Dan went to Keswick as a lad of seventeen. He had gratefully named his eldest son after the one through whom he had become a Christian.

Soon after Dan's return from Keswick, there came to Greenock a gentleman who was to play an important part in the next stage of Dan's life. His name was Mr. Somerset Gardiner. To many he was an object of amusement because of his eccentricities, that is, the unusual things he did. For example, he never wore coat, trousers or shoes. He preferred instead a kind of cloak and sandals, in which garb he travelled about the country wherever he felt that God wanted him to go. He spoke in churches and halls if he was invited, and in the open air if he was not. He trusted God to supply him with all that he needed.

As Dan prayed for daily guidance, he felt that God wanted him to leave his work as a bookkeeper and go with Mr. Gardiner. It was a most important step that he was taking. From then on for the rest of his life, Dan trusted God to lead him each day and to provide for all his needs.

Together, Dan Crawford and Somerset Gardiner travelled about the country, meeting many Christian folk and preaching the Gospel to those who knew not the Saviour. Among those whom they met was a Mrs. Shaw, of Wimbledon. She had had twelve sons, one of whom had longed to be a missionary, but had fallen ill and died. His last request to his parents was that they should find someone to take his place on the mission field and pay for his support. When the Shaws met Dan Crawford they felt at once that he was the one whom they should help in this way.

The two men next travelled north to Yorkshire. At Scarborough they preached to holiday makers on the sands and met a Mr. Corson, who invited them to his home in Harrogate. There they met a well-known missionary and explorer, Fred Arnot, who had just then reached England after a long trek across Africa. He had spent several months at the court of an African king called Mushidi, who ruled over Katanga, a very large area in what is now called the Belgian Congo. Fred Arnot told the seventeen-year-old Scottish lad of the many tribes who had never heard the Gospel and of how the great David Livingstone had longed to see the message carried to Katanga. Fifteen years had passed since Livingstone's death and still these tribes were unreached.

Fred Arnot was not connected with any of the great missionary societies. He trusted God to guide him and to supply his needs. His only link with other Christians was by means of a monthly paper, *Echoes of Service*, which published news from missionaries in all parts of the world. Such a way of life appealed strongly to Dan Crawford and he at once offered to return to Africa with Mr. Arnot.

Others responded to the appeal for workers until Mr. Arnot had about a dozen young men preparing to obey the command of Christ to preach the Gospel throughout the world. With him they travelled up and down England urging Christian folk to remember their responsibility towards those who had never heard of Christ. Among the places they visited was Bath, where Dan was invited to the home of a dentist named Mr. Tilsley, father of nine children, one of whom was destined to be the first white woman to live in Katanga, but you will hear more of her later on.

In March, 1889, the party left for Africa after an enthusiastic farewell meeting. Dan was not completely fit. He suffered from a troublesome cough which he knew meant that he had inherited the disease from which his father had died. But if he had only a year to live, he wanted to spend that year in the service of Christ and on behalf of the millions in Africa who knew nothing of God.

The thought that he might not have long to live only acted as a spur, urging him to use every moment of his time in furthering the cause of Christ. As it happened, he was to live for a good many years and it was to be twenty-two years before he again set foot in his homeland to see once more the mother who had readily given him to God's service, saying, "HE spared not His own Son."

III

A VENTURE OF FAITH

In the New Testament we read that Jesus told His followers not to be anxious about the things of this life, what they were going to eat and to drink and to wear. He promised that if they put God's Kingdom first all those necessary things would be theirs as well (read *Matthew* 6:33 for yourself and compare it with *Psalm* 34:10).

To Dan Crawford and his companions these promises meant exactly what they said. No one was going to pay them a salary, but they were the servants of the King of kings and they knew that He would provide for all their needs while they were engaged on His business.

At the end of March, 1889, they reached Lisbon, the capital of Portugal. As the part of Africa to which they were first going was a Portuguese colony, they had to go to Lisbon to board a ship. They spent a week in the city and Dan spent much of the time giving away gospel booklets and praying that God would use their message to reach the hearts of those who read them.

In like manner, on the ship, in spite of sea-sickness, he spoke to all about their need to know the Lord Jesus as their Saviour and Friend. The

ship called at two islands on the way to Africa.
The first was Madeira where the missionaries
landed and met local Christians. The other was
Principe, a tiny island about 300 miles off the
coast of Africa, but they did not land here
because of an outbreak of malaria. This is a
common disease in tropical countries, especially
near to rivers and swamps. It is spread by
mosquitoes which breed in the swamps. Little
was then known about the disease. It caused the
deaths of many missionaries before they could do
one half of all things they longed to do for Africa.

Two African boys came on board the ship at
Principe. They had been on the way to England
with a missionary of the Baptist Missionary
Society, but he had died of malaria and had been
buried at sea. The boys were, therefore, being
sent back to their homes. When Dan spoke to
them, he found to his joy that they had learned
to love the Lord Jesus.

A few days later he looked out upon the coast
of Africa, the continent for which he had prayed
so earnestly and where he was to spend most
of the rest of his life. For several days their vessel
sailed down the coast, calling at various ports.
One was Loanda, where Dr. Livingstone had
reached the coast at the end of his first great trek
across Africa. In his imagination Dan felt that
he could almost see the famous explorer and his
weary little company. He was always thrilled to
visit any place connected with that great man.

Thirty-eight days after leaving Lisbon, Dan

landed at Benguella. In those days there were no railways or roads into the interior of Africa. The aeroplane was undreamed of. The only method of travel was on foot, with a long string of porters to carry all the luggage. Distances which today can be covered in a few hours then took many months.

Of the fourteen who had set out from England with Fred Arnot, only three were to reach the Kingdom of Mushidi and the journey from the coast to his capital was to take eighteen months. It meant crossing rivers over which there were no bridges, cutting a way through thick jungle and passing through the territories of unfriendly native chiefs. It is hardly surprising to discover that their first difficulty was the finding of porters willing to leave their homes for several months and risk death at the hands of savage tribes.

Mr. Arnot had not expected this particular difficulty, for, when travelling alone in Africa, he had found it quite easy to collect a small band of carriers. Now, on horseback, he had to ride out to the villages in the surrounding country to find the men that he needed. At the end of about four months he had managed to get 160 men.

This may sound a large number to you, but there was a great deal to be carried, not only the personal belongings of the fourteen missionaries, but presents suitable for giving to the chiefs through whose lands they would pass and huge quantities of goods for barter. When we travel today in Africa or anywhere else we pay for what we need to buy with money. A large amount of paper money is light to carry. But the traveller in Africa sixty-five years ago would have found money quite useless. Instead he had to take long pieces of cloth and other goods which were both heavy and bulky. These things he exchanged for the food he needed to buy.

For three months after landing in Africa, Dan remained near the coast. Several times he was ill with malaria, but by July, 1889, he was well enough and ready to leave. With two other missionaries and six native porters he set off into the interior. Though he knew only too well the dangers that lay ahead and that he might never again see the great ocean over which he had come, he was singing for joy, sure that God was leading him on.

It was expected that the other missionaries would follow later, but three were soon to die and three others to return to England, victims of the unhealthy climate. By October, only eight remained of the fourteen who had landed five months earlier.

Among Dan Crawford's luggage as he set out on the long trek was a small copper kettle. It had been given to him before he left England and specially engraved upon it was the one word, "Ebenezer". I wonder if you know what that means. If not, look up the first book of *Samuel*, chapter 7, where you will read how Samuel set up a stone on a spot where a great battle had been won. He "called the name of it Ebenezer saying, hitherto hath the Lord helped us".

Dan's kettle, therefore, was to remind him every time he used it that up to that time the Lord had helped him. As long as the kettle lasted, it was one of his most treasured possessions.

As the little party travelled further inland, they saw lying beside the route discarded shackles and yokes which had been used to fetter slaves, for in those days slavery was still common and terrible cruelties were being committed against those unfortunate natives who were captured and sold as slaves.

Three days' journey brought them to the first village, where the natives sold them sweet potatoes and bananas. On one day they had to cross four streams, after first finding suitable places for crossing. In his diary Dan described how he cheerfully rode on his donkey into what looked like a shallow stream. When the water came up to his ankles, he put his feet on the donkey's neck, and then, just as the deepest point had been passed, he rolled off into the water!

After just over a week they reached the territory of King Ekwikwi, to whom they had to give a handsome present—a large quantity of cloth— before he would allow them to go on.

Next came the River Keve, too deep for the donkey to wade through as it had done at all the previous streams. The crossing had to be made, therefore, in a tiny boat, just large enough for two people to squeeze into. The boat, made of bark, leaked badly, so that, Dan tells us, the water was "as much in the boat as the boat in the water". It must have been an alarming experience, but his sense of humour helped him out. "You feel as safe," he wrote, "as if you had put to sea in a wash-tub and about as dry."

After ten days' journey they reached a place called Bailundu, where they met up with Mr. and Mrs. Arnot, who were about to return to the coast, while Dan was to continue further into the heart of Africa.

It was at this point that news reached Mr. Arnot that a certain slave trader was travelling into the interior with a large caravan. It would be possible for a missionary—though sworn enemy of slavery—to join this caravan. Whoever did so would be able to reach many tribes still living in the darkness of their heathen faiths, far from any place where the glorious light of the Gospel had ever shone. The question was: whom should he send to take advantage of this wonderful opportunity? Dan Crawford—still only nineteen —seemed too young; in any case most of his personal belongings were still back at the coast; he had no personal possessions except the bundle which he carried himself. While Arnot asked God to guide them, Dan became sure that God was calling him to this work.

The following day the two men separated, Arnot returning to the coast, while Dan made preparations for the next stage of his long journey. He spent many hours making candles from a wax obtained by the natives from the honeycomb and chewed for hours to make it suitable for candles.

With him were the six native carriers who had
come with him from the coast and were prepared
to stay with him on this next adventure. One
carried the cloth needed for barter; another a box
containing medicines and books, "especially
The One Book", Dan wrote. I expect you can
guess which one he meant. The others carried
food and bedding and a tent.

He still had his brave little donkey. On the
first day out the poor creature fell unexpectedly
into a deep stream, but swam safely to the bank.
Dan was really proud of it.

A sight which interested him greatly was that
of the ant hills. The huge domes, with their
networks of galleries made him praise God who
had given such great skill to these tiny creatures.
After a few days' journey, he reached the home
of an aged Portuguese gentleman, who had spent
nearly all his life in Africa and had been the first
to tell Mr. Arnot of the tribes in the interior who
had never heard the Gospel. At least Dan reached
the village in which the old gentleman lived. His
home had been burned down a few days before
and he was using a tiny hut. He was most
grateful to the young Scotsman for bringing him
a box of much needed goods. Awaiting Dan in
this village was a message urging him to hurry
if he wished to join the travellers who were
leaving for the interior. He, therefore, pressed on
at full speed, but even so arrived four days too
late to join the caravan.

It was necessary for him to learn a very important lesson—the need for patience. It is always more difficult to be patient when we are young and Dan was to wait about twelve months before his journey could be continued. For a time he made his home with a Canadian missionary in a small mud hut and spent his days studying the language which he had to master before he could make known the Gospel of Christ effectively.

IV

LEARNING TO "THINK BLACK"

NEAR Chisamba, where Dan Crawford was to spend the next few months of his life lived a tribe called the Biheans, an intelligent and healthy folk, who had made themselves rich out of the many caravans passing through their land. Their chief was named Chindundumuna, meaning, "The terror who makes the earth tremble". At first he was unfriendly to the missionaries, so much so that it appeared that their lives were in danger. They were very careful not to use weapons. Instead they put their trust in God and gained a reputation for their peaceful-ness. "It is become quite a proverb all round," wrote Dan, " 'They don't fight: their sword is their Book'."

As he struggled to learn the language, Dan realized that he must spend much time talking with the natives. In that way only, he believed, could he really learn to speak and to think as they did. He felt that this last point was very important indeed. He must think like the Africans thought. Only then could he understand them fully and gain their confidence. Later on we shall see how well he achieved this object and when he came to write the story of his wonderful adventures, he called the book, *Thinking Black*.

Having decided what he must do he acted quickly. He thanked the Canadian missionary for his kindness and hospitality. Then he moved his few belongings into an African hut, where he could live exactly as did the natives. There was no chimney, so that, in the evenings, when he lit his little fire, the hut was filled with smoke. His furniture consisted of a narrow shelf-like bed, a low stool and a grass mat. He lived on the same kind of food as the natives, but did not have to worry about buying it for he was presented with food by every family in the village.

Each morning, at about five o'clock, he was awakened by the noise of the women pounding their corn. He marvelled at the way these African women worked. At about seven o'clock they went off into the fields where they worked all morning, many of them with babies tied on their backs. At midday or early afternoon they returned to the village carrying baskets of ripe corn on their heads. Next they would go to the brook for the daily supply of water which they also carried on their heads in black, earthen pitchers three feet tall. From then on until it grew dark, they worked away at their corn, pounding it into flour.

In the evenings Dan would often sit with the men of the village around a camp fire. There they would talk, Dan practising the language he was slowly learning. As soon as he could make himself understood clearly, he told his hearers of God's great love in sending His Son to die for them on Calvary. The conversation would be interrupted from time to time by young children bringing their fathers' suppers. Each child would bring two neat little baskets, one containing a kind of porridge made from Indian corn, the other a tasty dish made from a local plant, in which, occasionally, some meat was also mixed. These hours of chatting about his Master over the camp fire—"gossiping the Gospel" he called it—were among the happiest of his life.

One day he found a native in great distress because his gun had fallen into a deep part of the river. Dan offered to dive for it and the native promised him a pig if he could recover the gun. Many times he dived into the water but could not find it. Eventually it was found about fifty yards from the part where Dan had been searching. He was disappointed, for he had tasted no meat for many months and had looked forward to a meal of roast pork!

During these months of waiting, Dan visited many other villages. He travelled for several days' journey in every direction, making known the

Good News to hundreds who had never heard it before. In one village he was offered a house if he would stay and teach the people more, but he was very sure that God was calling him to work further inland and decided that he must not accept their kind offer.

By May, 1890, after nine months of waiting, the way began to open for him to go on further. Permission was given by the local chief for carriers to be recruited to form a caravan. The goods belonging to two missionaries who were in the interior had come up from the coast. Two more missionaries, Mr. Lane and Mr. Thompson, had arrived and were ready for the venture. Though older than Dan Crawford, they were quite happy to go under his leadership, partly because he was more familiar with the language than they were and partly because of his standing with the natives who looked upon him as the senior because he had a beard, while the others were clean-shaven. Hair does not grow on the faces of Africans until they are middle aged. In consequence they regarded a bearded person as senior to those without beards.

V

THE PATH OF THE SLAVE TRADERS

ONE of the first obstacles they met was the
Kwanza River, the crossing of which was a
memorable stage in the journey of the three
missionaries and their caravan of porters. Lane
and Thompson went over first to receive the
loads, while Dan stayed on the nearer side to
direct the crossing. An aged chief, who came
down to the crossing to watch them, was puzzled
to find that they were not traders. He had never
heard of white men who were interested in anything else. Busy as he was seeing to the loads,
Dan found time to explain the purpose of their
coming to Africa, to make known their loving God.

The canoes in which the crossing was made
were simply hollowed out tree trunks. So
frightened were the natives at making the journey
that they huddled together in the bottom of the
boat.

The crossing of rivers was always difficult. The
frail craft could easily be capsized by crocodiles
or by the movements of those who were in it.
There was another very human problem. The
ferryman, as often as not, would agree to ferry
the travellers' goods across for a certain price and
then, when the boat was in midstream, he would

demand more, threatening to overturn the canoe
if he did not get it.

In this case the ferryman found he had met his
match in Dan Crawford. Pushing off with a
valuable load, he kept close to the shore and
began to demand much more than had been
agreed. Dan refused. The ferryman then
threatened to capsize the boat, but Dan took one
leap, landed in the vessel, clung to the legs of the
rogue and told him that he intended to hang on
until all the goods were safely across!

On another occasion the experience he had
gained living among the natives came in useful.
The chief, who ruled the crossing, was saying that
he was not responsible for the loss of a load which
his men had deliberately tipped into the water.
Dan replied by quoting an African proverb
which he had learned when teaching himself to
"think black":

> "Though, in crossing, the crocodile he gets your
> stuff,
> 'Tis the ferryman pays and must pay you
> enough."

When the chief found that Dan had lived as an
African, and had taken the trouble to learn their
speech and their proverbs, he was so delighted
that he paid for the goods which had been lost.
"Then it was," wrote Dan, "that I learned the
cash value of proverbs in Africa and I have been
collecting them ever since." Many of these
proverbs and sayings he used when he was
preaching to drive home important truths.

One day the three missionaries were confronted with a sad and tragic sight, one which, happily, can be seen in Africa no longer. It was a large caravan of slaves—800 of them, of all ages, from old men to tiny toddlers crawling along as best they could. Many were young mothers with babies. One baby had been born that very morning. At the sight of their owner cruelly beating one poor girl who was struggling to keep up with the rest, Dan attacked him with his stick; but the man did not wait—he fled into the bush!

Sometimes as they journeyed, their stock of food ran low. Once, when they were very short, they met a party of travellers who had been robbed and were glad to exchange some *ombowi* for the goods which the missionaries carried to use as money. This *ombowi* was a favourite food of Dan's: it reminded him of bread and cheese! Actually it was made from the manioc root, the plant from which we get tapioca.

In other places they were able to buy bananas, tomatoes and sweet potatoes, according to what grew most plentifully in the district where they were. For money they used cloth and salt. Tobacco and gunpowder were often asked for, but the missionaries rarely parted with their gunpowder, knowing that more likely than not it would be used for taking human life. They occasionally gave some away when sure that it was required for hunting.

One kindly chief to whom they gave a present, sent them, in return, a large fowl and some baskets of meal, for which they were very grateful indeed. Another chief sent a goat and some flour in exchange for eight handkerchiefs.

There were other gifts or acts of intended kindness which were less welcome, as, for instance, that of the chief who sent a band of minstrels to dance and sing for them. The minstrels began their noise in the early evening and kept it up until breakfast time, so that the three missionaries were quite unable to sleep. In the morning the chief came to them himself with the more acceptable present of a sheep.

When one of their men died, the other porters took great pains to prevent the news from becoming known in the village near which they were encamped. They dug a hole inside a tent and buried their comrade there. Had news of the death reached the village, they would have had to pay a heavy fine and would possibly have been delayed for weeks.

The difficulties and the dangers of the journey caused the missionaries to put their trust in God rather than in the guns which they carried. When a chief tried to bar their way, they prayed to God and then told the chief that they intended to reach a place further on. When he saw their determination, he gave his permission provided they gave him salt and twelve yards of cloth.

After about five weeks' travelling, the party came to a great sandy desert called the Kifumadzi Flat. They were in a part of Africa which at that itme had been little explored and the extent of the desert was not known. On the first day they walked for five hours in soft sand in hopes of finding water. In the end they dug for water and came upon some after about an hour of digging. It looked too dirty to drink, but after they had waited for the sediment to settle it was quite clear.

On the third day they reached a river, beside which grew many kinds of vegetation, a pleasant change after the desert. After following the bank for some way, they found a good place to cross, where the river was both narrow and shallow. To their surprise native fishermen appeared and sold them some fish.

Beyond the river their way lay across a grassy plain into the country of an important chief named Kangombe. They found him sitting on a skin beneath a large tree surrounded by his counsellors. His face bore a cunning look and he was treated with very great respect. The present offered by the missionaries was quietly returned to them with a demand for a larger one!

Just over a week after leaving Kangombe, they reached a large town called Nakandundu, the inhabitants of which appeared to make a good living selling the produce of their gardens to the many travellers who came their way.

Owing to the dangers of travel between Nakandundu and the coast, travellers would usually wait in this town until a large and powerful caravan could be collected together for the journey, for small parties were more likely to be set upon, robbed and killed. Often a caravan would be hundreds strong before it set out; sometimes the number of the men would run into thousands. The ruler of this important centre was a woman, Queen Nakandundu. So many rings and bangles did she wear that the missionaries could hardly see her arms, legs or fingers.

They stayed here for about a week and it was here that they paid their men—twenty-four yards of cloth to each one. It was the payment for which they had agreed to come, but they now grumbled that it was not enough. Raising their voices in loud protest, they said they would not go a step further. The missionaries took stock of the cloth they had left, counted up the number of days' journey ahead of them—about four weeks—and decided that if they gave them any more they would themselves soon be "penniless"! When the porters saw that their protests were having no effect, they quietened down and cheerfully prepared to continue the journey.

Another problem was that the porters would try to buy slaves for themselves if they had the chance. Already the missionaries had set one such slave free. Now they discovered that while in Nakandundu the porters had secretly bought a number of slaves, among them a little girl of ten. Dan thought he had never seen anyone look so sad as this unhappy child. As the journey continued the party came near to the home from which she had been carried away in a cruel raid.

Someone recognized her and took the news to her father. Though a poor man he was ready to pay any price to get his daughter back. In the end he obtained her in exchange for two slaves, twelve fowls and a gun.

Another porter had purchased a baby girl, too young even to walk. Dan feared that the child would be clubbed to death by its heartless owner. He, therefore, redeemed her himself for thirty-two yards of cloth. "So here I am with a little child in my care," he wrote, "to instruct in the way she should go."

On November 1st, after about ten weeks of travel, they came to the top of a hill from where stretched before them a great valley and beyond that a range of mountains, the border of the land which was their destination. But their difficulties were not yet over. They had trouble with the chief at the village near which they had to cross the river. He wanted them to give him a gun, but they refused. Once again the determination of the missionaries overcame the opposition. He accepted their gift and allowed them to pass.

The way was now clear to the capital of Mushidi, a very powerful ruler, the king of a huge area of Africa. It was Mushidi who had invited Mr. Arnot to send missionaries to his country; not that he wanted his people to become Christians, but it added to his own importance to have white men living at his court. Two missionaries, Mr. Swan and Mr. Faulkner, were already there, and to them Dan sent forward messengers with the news that their party was approaching. We can imagine the joy of Swan and Faulkner at the arrival of these reinforcements and their thankfulness to God that the long and dangerous journey had been safely completed.

A few days later the three newly arrived missionaries were received in audience by Mushidi. Putting on the cleanest clothes they could find and the stiff collars they had brought with them for this very occasion, they found themselves being led through an avenue of tall poles. At the top of each pole there appeared to be a white ball. Suddenly, with a shock, they realized that the white balls were human skulls. Outside Mushidi's hut sat three fierce-looking men—his chief executioners. Hardly a day passed on which these three men were not called upon to murder men and women who had offended their king.

Mushidi received the missionaries kindly and accepted their gifts—lengths of cloth, seventy-two handkerchiefs, a silk robe, eight yards of turban silk and other things. He at once tried on the robe and was delighted at his appearance. He asked them to sing to him and to eat with him. He was pleased to find that Dan spoke well enough to hold direct conversation with him without an interpreter.

We may try to imagine Dan's feelings as he talked to the aged chief. This Mushidi, who seemed so kind, was daily ordering the most dreadful cruelties to be committed. Writing to friends at home, Dan asked them to pray for him, that he might be as "bold as a lion" and soon learn to speak the language well, so that he could preach the Gospel of God's love in this place where hatred and cruelty were the order of the day. He also asked them to pray for Mushidi, that he might become a Christian.

VI

A YEAR WITH MUSHIDI

LIFE in Mushidi's capital must have been strange to the missionaries. It was so completely different from anything they had ever known before.

To begin with Mushidi was a very proud man, so proud that he expected those around him to treat him almost as though he were God. Then he had a very large number of wives. Not all of them lived with him, or even lived in the capital. Many of them were governors of distant areas of his dominions. But it was the custom that the more important a man was, the more wives he would possess—and I have used the word possess because he owned those wives in much the same way that in other lands men own flocks of sheep and herds of cattle. We do not know exactly how many wives he had—probably about 600 and maybe as many as 700.

You would think that with so many he would

have been satisfied. But oh no! He wanted a *white* wife to add to their number and he had asked Mr. Arnot to find him one. Of course, Mr. Arnot refused, but as soon as Mushidi heard that Mr. Arnot was back in Africa with two white women, only one of whom was his (Arnot's) wife, he jumped to the conclusion that the missionary had changed his mind and had brought him a white wife. You will not be surprised to hear that Mr. Swan wrote to Mr. Arnot to tell him that it would be unwise for an unmarried woman missionary to come to Mushidi's capital.

Over a period of many years, Mushidi had built up a vast empire in Africa, with himself at the head. He had discovered that white men possessed a powerful weapon, by means of which they could kill from a distance. In order to obtain guns and gunpowder, he had traded immense quantities of ivory, copper and slaves. His men had found a route from the very heart of the great continent to the west coast, and long caravans of slaves and trading goods had crossed and re-crossed many, many times. Thus Mushidi had grown rich and powerful. Moreover, Katanga, the land over which he ruled, had much more wealth to offer. Many minerals were to be found there—iron, tin, gold, diamonds and uranium. The rivers teemed with fish and the soil was for the most part fertile, so that good crops could be grown.

On the other hand his capital had been allowed to grow so big that there was not enough water for the thousands who lived there, while every tree for miles around had long since been cut down for fuel.

He believed himself to be the greatest monarch in Africa and as such should kill the greatest number of people. That is why such dreadful slaughter went on around him. Mr. Arnot had protested most strongly about it when he first came to Mushidi's about four years before Dan Crawford's arrival. All that Mushidi did was to give him a hut, from which he could not see the murders being committed!

The bodies of the wretched victims of this cruelty were thrown out into the bush. They were not buried properly. Now you know that you will get your house overrun with mice if you leave crumbs and bits of food about. In Africa dead bodies which are not buried attract wild animals, such as lions, leopards and hyenas. The result was that these beasts were often prowling around close to the capital. Once, one of Mushidi's wives was killed by a leopard. All that he did was to order poison to be put in the body so that the next wild beast that came along would be killed.

As he grew older he used to have frequent fits of anger, during which he would order large numbers of his subjects to be executed. Several times Dan Crawford himself caused these out-bursts, because of his bold protests at the wicked-ness that was going on and his firm refusal to help Mushidi to get more guns and gunpowder. More than once he expected to hear the fatal words, "Die, son of a dog of a white man." At the utterance of this phrase, the executioners would have quickly killed Dan as they did the other victims.

But God watched over His servant in that far-off corner of Africa where no help could be expected from any European power. In his quieter moments, Mushidi thought so much of the young missionary that he advised his counsellors to make Dan their chief after he (Mushidi) had died.

For 404 days these two men, Dan Crawford and Mushidi, were in frequent contact with each other. The one was a servant of all that was evil, pursuing a course of murder, cruelty and wickedness too dreadful for me to describe in detail; the other was the servant of the living God, seeking to spread love where there was hate, joy where there was misery, faith where there was fear.

Then there were other forces at work outside the power of either the Scottish missionary or the heathen king. Some of the peoples under Mushidi's rule were in revolt; Arabs were raiding his rich caravans on the route between Katanga and the coast; and certain white men were greedily planning to gain control of the riches of his land, especially the gold which they believed was there.

Within a few days of reaching Mushidi's capital, Dan was studying hard at the language. He and Mr. Swan lived together after the other three missionaries, two of them seriously ill, had returned westwards. As Dan learned the speech, so he practised, preaching the Gospel wherever he found groups of people ready to listen. By thus talking much with the natives, he learned rapidly and astonished the older missionary by his mastery over the language.

He had enjoyed wonderfully good health on the journey, but shortly after reaching Mushidi's he had attacks of fever. He hated to be in bed, unable to do anything, and was about again as soon as possible. A month after his arrival, he had his twenty-first birthday. There can be few missionaries who have celebrated their coming-of-age on the mission field. Sometimes he had breakfast with Mushidi. Here is his own description of such an occasion: "We squat, tailor fashion, round a wooden tray. Water is brought before we commence to eat and poured over our hands. No knives or forks. The food is generally a mountain of mush and goat's meat."

Sometimes an incident would occur which gave the missionaries hope for better things. One day Mushidi was angrily rebuking three men who had come with a message. Swan and Crawford were expecting to hear at any moment the fearful words, "Die, sons of the dust!" Instead the king suddenly said, "I am getting like the white men here, ashamed to cut off heads, or else I would cut off yours." Their lives were spared.

About six or seven months after his arrival, Dan moved out to a more pleasant spot. The move was made at Mushidi's suggestion and he himself intended to follow them. The place chosen was more healthy, partly because there were no corpses lying around and partly because there was a good supply of fresh, clean water.

Dan was learning no fewer than seven languages. He was soon able to write hymns in these new languages; these were sung to the tunes of well-known English hymns. When he had used up all his ink, he made more out of the bark of one of the local trees. When his last nib broke, his two pencils became very precious; and when his home-made candles were all used, he filled a coffee pot with a kind of oil and stuffed a piece of flannel shirt down the spout. This acted as a wick and provided him with a dim light.

In order to keep their larder well stocked the missionaries had to go out hunting. On leaving England, Dan had not felt it was important to buy a good rifle. But he made up for the poor quality of his weapon by training himself to become an excellent shot. The meat obtained in this way not only provided them with food but also with money; for they could exchange it for other things they needed, such as flour, honey and oil.

Dan always used his gun from his left shoulder, as he was left-handed, though he taught himself to write and draw with both hands.

In a letter to his mother, Dan wrote an exciting description of the killing of a hippopotamus. Hiding himself in the tall grass on the river bank he waited for the right moment to pull the trigger. "Along they came," he wrote, "right under the muzzle of my rifle, only about twenty yards away. In extra glee one of them raises himself out of the water, giving me the opportunity of putting 380 grams of lead right into his heart. Crack! goes my rifle. And Roa-oa-oar! goes the hippo. Down he plunges; but an hour or so afterwards the dead body rises on the opposite side." Early the next morning, two of his men swam over to the other side and towed it back, just reaching the shore in time to escape from a crocodile which appeared on the scene.

Swimming in African rivers is usually something in the nature of an adventure. One day after a swim, Dan wrote in his diary, "Good-bye to bathing in streams with which I am unacquainted! Today when I was in the water a formidable water-snake fairly chased me, coming on with head erect like the prow of an old viking galley."

Towards the end of 1891 news reached Mushidi that some white men were coming to his capital from the east. It had been foretold years before that he would die at the hand of a white man from the east. However, he did not suspect that they intended him any harm. They arrived with a band of soldiers and told Mushidi that he must never again kill anyone. Realizing then that these newcomers meant to take away from him all his great power, he fled from his capital, but the men followed him and on December 20th of that year one of them shot and killed this powerful chief. We cannot feel very sorry for him, for he

was one of the wickedest and cruellest rulers
there have ever been. His lands were soon afterwards to be absorbed into a great state, the head
of which would be the King of the Belgians.
If you look at a map of Africa, you will see that a
large area in the centre of the Continent is called
the Belgian Congo. It is so large that England,
Scotland and Wales could be fitted into it ten
times over. The south-east corner of it is Katanga
and is the part over which Mushidi ruled.

For 404 days Dan Crawford had lived at the
court of this cruel heathen monarch. Mushidi's
sudden death found the young Scottish missionary
—he was just twenty-two—in a position of
enormous responsibility at one of the most important moments of Africa's history.

VII

GATHERER OF THE PEOPLE

FOLLOWING the murder of Mushidi, there was a
great deal of suffering mainly because the people
were terribly short of food. Hundreds died of
hunger, while those who lived wandered off in
search of food. Mushidi had not allowed Dan to
travel freely. Now it was possible for him to go
where he wished. He followed the people, telling
them of the Lord Jesus, the Bread of Life, who
alone could satisfy the hunger of their souls.

In the Spring, things improved and Dan was able to write that there were plenty of sweet potatoes, tomatoes, beans and peanuts. Living with him were two small boys whom he had rescued. One of them, Segunda by name, though only seven, was an excellent little cook. Once shown how to cook anything, he was able to do it himself without further instruction. He made meat pies and pastry, even putting little bits of decoration on the top like we do. Frying was done in buffalo fat.

The other boy, Sankuru, was not so bright at first. This was hardly surprising, for the poor boy's father had been killed by one of Mushidi's executioners. When Dan first saw him he was sitting beside his father's skull in the presence of Mushidi.

Dan's companion, Mr. Swan, had returned to the coast and his place had been taken by a Mr. Thompson. They were the only missionaries within hundreds of miles. In June, 1892, they set out on a journey southwards to carry the message of God's love to other tribes who had never heard. In the mountains, they came upon folk who stored their food in caves far beyond the reach of those who would rob them of it. They lived mainly on fish which they caught in the mountain streams, roots, fruit and honey. Among these strange people the missionaries received a friendly welcome. They were the first white men ever to visit that part of Africa and rejoiced that God had chosen them to be His messengers.

One day the missionaries climbed up to a

mountain village and preached to about 200 people. They were thrilled to think that they were singing God's praises where only the sounds of devil worship had been heard before.

When they returned to their base, a place called Lofoi, they found that letters from home had arrived. Soon they were planning another journey, this time in the opposite direction. In his diary Dan wrote:

MOTTO: "I bring you good tidings of great joy" (*Luke* 2:10).

RESOLVE: "To preach the Gospel, not where Christ was named" (*Romans* 15:20).

Taking with them five boys, all under fourteen and one of them only five, they set out, but Mr. Thompson was taken ill on the second night and had to return to Lofoi. The great heat made Dan ill for a time. He had to lie down by the roadside, but kindly natives found him and carried him in a kind of hammock to the nearby village.

He was able to continue the journey after a couple of days' rest. Sankuru, the seven-year-old boy, swam across the river to fetch Dan's canoe from the further side. They went on until they came to two tiny villages where the people lived mainly on fish. Dan ate some before he discovered that their method of catching fish was to throw poisonous fruit into the stream. However, he was none the worse and travelled on the next day, a memorable one, for three lions suddenly jumped out of the bush close to their party. They had a remarkable escape, probably because the lions were not hungry, having just finished off a large water buck, but Dan felt that God had protected them in the moment of danger.

As he travelled on, the natives gazed in astonishment at the first white man they had ever seen. They listened with open mouths to the Gospel message which Dan preached. They could not understand how God could love those who had so ill-treated His Son. To them the slightest supposed wrong was an excuse to plan revenge.

One night, after Dan had told the Gospel story, he heard the chief of the village calling out, "Who was it who came down to deliver us? I forget." After a time someone called out that it was Moses, for Dan had told them the story of Moses delivering the Israelites from Egypt. Then one of Dan's boys interrupted. "No, you're wrong," he called out, "Moses was just a man like ourselves, but Jesus had no sin and was God's only begotten Son."

Dan came one day to the village of a chief named Katanga, where he found, imprisoned in a tiny hovel and almost starved to death, an old woman. She had been a sister of the great Mushidi, but she had been captured. Now she implored Dan to help her. Deeply moved by the misery of this once powerful woman, he pleaded with the chief to release her. Katanga did not want to give up so valuable a prisoner, but at last he gave in to the pleas of the Scottish lad whose eyes blazed with anger at the cruelties he saw around him.

The old woman was very grateful to Dan, and her people welcomed her back with a joyful exhibition of yelling, dancing and singing, crying out that she who had been lost was found again, she who had been dead was alive again. The following year, while at work in the fields, she was killed and eaten by a lion.

So grateful to Dan were her people for his part in rescuing her that they gave him a seven-year-old boy, named Katapila. Dan at once set the little slave free and gained for himself another devoted young follower.

Arriving back at Lofoi, Dan learned from Mr. Thompson that his hut had nearly been burned down. He would have had little to lose even if the whole hut had been destroyed. His most valuable possessions were his Bible and the papers containing the beginnings of his translation of the New Testament into the native tongue. These he always carried with him. He had no English food and no cloth for trading or material for making his clothes. In fact his personal belongings were very few indeed. He had sold his sheets to obtain food, had made his towels into clothes for his boys and his blankets were so worn that he had to sleep near the fire to keep warm. His poverty worried him very little as we see from a letter he wrote about this time: "Thank God, though such luxuries as tea, coffee and cocoa have to come from Europe and may be six months in transit, the joy of God comes from heaven and may be mine in a moment."

In a letter to his mother, written on New Year's Day, 1893, he wrote that he had been without tea, coffee and cocoa for seven months. It was over a year since any supplies had reached him.

At about this time Dan was given a new name. Up to now the Africans had called him Kalawfwa, which was the nearest they could say to Crawford. Now, however, they began to call him Konga Vantu, meaning "Gatherer of the People." This was because of the part he played in gathering the folk together again after the scattering which had followed the death of Mushidi.

Dan now set about the building of a larger house for himself at Lofoi. In doing so he hoped that before long more missionaries would reach there. Then they could occupy this house, while he could go out to evangelize the surrounding villages.

But it was a very wet year and one dark night everyone in Lofoi was awakened by a terrifying sound—the approach of floods. The people ran from their huts and climbed ant hills and trees in their frantic efforts to escape. The two missionaries spent the rest of the night on the roof of Dan's house. His boys were in a nearby tree. Thankful that their lives were spared, they sang:

"God we thank Thee,
Thou who lovest us;
Thou givest us our life
And all good things."

When day dawned, after what Dan described as "the longest night I have ever passed in my life," there was a vast lake of flood water all around them. It was three days before the waters began to go down, leaving behind so much mud that it was impossible to get about. Little was left of the houses and most of Dan's simple possessions had been swept away, but he uttered no word of complaint. Their lives had been spared and he felt the nearness of God. "Our Jesus hath done all things well," he wrote.

There were other disasters too—an epidemic of smallpox and a disease among the cattle which was carried by tsetse flies. One day Dan was chatting with some natives when he saw a huge black cloud in the sky. It was moving towards them. When it came nearer, they heard a sound like a rushing wind and realized that it was a swarm of locusts, insects like large grasshoppers which settle on the land and strip it of everything growing there. Fortunately there were no crops in the fields at the time and again Dan gave thanks to God for sparing them from utter disaster.

VIII

SOWING THE SEED

DAN CRAWFORD was following in the steps of two great missionary explorers, David Livingstone and Fred Arnot. Both had blazed a trail into the heart of Africa. Both had sowed the seed of God's Word, but neither of them had seen the harvest. It was left largely to those who came after them to see the Africans of the tropical forests begin to turn their backs on the cruel ways of witchcraft and heathenism to follow the way of Christ.

As Dan went out on his journeys, this thought of seed sowing was uppermost in his mind. He would call his journey "running a seed furrow"— that is, preparing the ground for the actual sowing.

Already we have heard how from Lofoi he journeyed north and south. His next journey was to the east. There were no fewer than twenty-four in his party when he set out, including several women travelling with their husbands. Some were going to visit relatives in villages to which Dan was going. He was in much pain from neuralgia, but was determined to push on in spite of this. Great care was needed, for ant bears had dug holes in the path along which they were travelling. A broken leg could easily have resulted from an unwary step. Their route lay first along a river valley, then up into mountains where the temperature was several degrees below freezing point. Imagine how cold they must have felt after the heat of the valley.

After a day or two on the mountains they emerged from the forest to find a wonderful view before them. Stretching away into the distance was Lake Mweru, a lake as big as Cornwall. In the valley were a number of villages, and to these Dan went with his message. As there was an epidemic of smallpox he made strict rules that those with him were not to borrow anything from the villagers.

There followed a journey through grass ten feet tall. "You can no more see the trail than if you were blind," he wrote, "for the overhead grass is tangled and matted above it; you must push forward with your feet below to feel for a foothold, and then drag your body after them by main force." As they pushed their way through, needle pointed grass seeds showered down upon them. He learned later that the lake had once covered the part where this long grass grew. It had dried up, however, and in places crops were being grown where once there had been water.

After crossing a wide river, the Luapula, in rather frail canoes, Dan and his party reached the town of a chief known as the Kazembe. This chief considered himself so important that no one was even allowed to eat at the same time

as himself. Nor would he "lower" himself to shake
hands with white men. A huge blanket was held
up to hide him from prying eyes at meal times.
When he had finished eating, a drum was
sounded loudly as a signal to everyone else that
they could eat!

Dan and his friends were received amid a tre-
mendous noise of beating drums. "The drumming
is deafening," he wrote, "round drums, square
drums and angular drums, all swelling the din."
The Kazembe had been given splendid gifts by a
British trading company, beside which Dan's
present of sixteen yards of wide calico and a
blanket seemed small, but he was not ashamed
to offer it, for he was also offering the African
chief a treasure greater than any to be found on
earth. "I was a King's ambassador," he says,
"offering him the riches of heaven." Dan soon
explained why he had come, preaching the
Gospel and denouncing the wickedness of the
slave trade and cruel practices such as the lopping
off of ears and hands.

When they reached the village of a chief named
Mbayo, Dan's seven-year-old boy Sankuru was
re-united with his mother. He had been taken
from his home by one of Mushidi's raiding
parties. Relatives offered to buy him back,
thinking that he was still a slave, but the lad clung
to the missionary, knowing that he would be
happier and safer with the white man than he
would be if he returned to his native village,
where he would be at everyone's beck and call.

Dan's party was very well treated here and loaded with more food than they could manage to eat. When they left, the chief himself acted as their guide to the next village, on the way to which Dan shot a boar for their supper. They were again well received and Dan was the first white man ever seen there.

The next two or three days were spent travelling across really rough country. They had to lift their feet high to avoid tripping over roots. The long grass they walked through made them wet and their feet were sore from tramping over uneven ground. Remembering his Master's sufferings, Dan wrote in his diary, "All for Jesus who trod the thorny path for me."

At times Dan was delayed by the natives with him, for they would wander off at the sound of the honey guide, a little bird which feeds on bees. It has a curious habit of calling out for human help when it finds honey. The natives would go off in the direction of the sound, help themselves to the honey and leave the bees to the bird. Sometimes Dan had to wait an hour or more when this happened, but at least there was the consolation that he received a share of the pure and delicious honey.

On the way back to Lofoi, across the mountain range, they went down by a route so dangerous that Dan had to take off his boots in order to get a better grip with his feet. Here is his own description: "I continued the descent on my back, clutching at tufts of grass and tiny ledges of rock for a handhold. However careful anyone was, stones would get dislodged and bump down on those before. In the mercy of God we reached the bottom at last, bathed all our bruises in the river and pushed on for a village which we reached near nightfall."

IX

DAN FINDS A NEW HOME

ON his return to Lofoi, Dan was warmly welcomed. The people gathered around him, overjoyed to see him again. They called him "father", though many of them were old enough to be *his* father or even grandfather. What pleased him most was that they regarded him not as a stranger from a far-off land but as one of themselves. He received many presents from his visitors and was deeply touched by these tokens of their love for him. He was now sure that before long many of these lovable folk would turn their backs on heathenism and follow the Lord Jesus Christ.

The people came to him with their problems and found in him a ready listener and a wise counsellor. Patiently he would listen for hours to what they had to say and then he would tell them of the loving Saviour who could set them free from the bondage of sin.

His need of trading goods was so great by now

that he decided he would have to shoot an elephant in order to sell its ivory tusks to obtain the material he needed for clothes. He had just gone off to do so when some goods arrived.

To his mother he wrote: "I really never need anything here, for God supplies it all." He trusted God to supply him with what he needed in the same simple way that boys and girls trust their parents to clothe and feed them.

One day Tapila, one of his boys, laid the table and then inquired what he was going to eat. Dan pointed upwards to show that he was trusting God for his next meal. Indeed there was no food in the larder. "Just then," he writes, "as though in heaven a dinner bell had gone for my meal appeared an old woman . . . with a basket of whitest flour, and, hard on her heels, came someone else with a leg of venison." He was able to boast that his little family of boys were all well fed and he looked forward to the time when they would become true Christians and go forth as evangelists among their own folk.

The arrival of trading goods and supplies gave Dan the opportunity to repay those natives who had been most kind to him when he had nothing at all to give them in exchange. He had made a careful note of every basket of flour and vegetables that had been given him in readiness for the time when he could show his gratitude.

With the goods had come letters from home with the news that for the time being no more missionaries were coming. This caused Dan to work all the harder himself. After a few weeks at Lofoi, he was off again—to explore the area around Lake Mweru.

The first few villages through which his journey lay were places where he was known and he was given a royal welcome. A number of people, wanting to travel in the direction Dan was going, joined his little caravan. All were welcome, for he could tell them more about the Lord whom he served.

Once more he had to climb the mountains over which he had had such a dangerous journey a few weeks before. This time he saw something of the natives who lived on the plateau and the pains they took to prevent strangers from finding their path. They would cut down trees and crawl in various directions to lay false trails. On the real path they would carefully cover up their tracks so that no one could tell where they had been. Fortunately, Dan had a good guide with him, so good that his party was able to climb the mountains and reach the native village before its inhabitants knew that strangers were coming. They looked unfriendly until they saw that Dan was unarmed. Then they brought him welcome gifts of fat fowls and good eggs. Many people were living among the rocks. During the day they came from all around to see the man with the white skin and by evening they were all his firm friends.

After a day's rest among these folk, Dan led his party down the eastern side of the mountains to the village of a chief named Chilolo, whom he had visited before. He asked Chilolo if he remembered what had been told him about God. Yes, he replied, he remembered and had spoken of it often to his children. For four days Dan stayed in the village, freely preaching the Gospel. "There is no chief," he wrote, "who is not on terms of friendship with me, the said friendship having been made and sustained when I had not a yard of calico to give to any of them."

At least he knew that their friendliness was not due to what they could get out of him. He was, however, much saddened to learn later that on the day after he had left one of these friendly villages, it was attacked by a cruel raider called Shimba (the Lion). The huts were burned down and the chief was carried away a prisoner in chains as punishment for his kindness to the white man.

Next, Dan crossed Lake Mweru at the point near where the River Luapula flows into it. He carefully measured the width of the river and found it to be 592 yards. He then found himself following a route along which Livingstone had once passed. Livingstone's map proved useful and Dan found that it was very accurate.

The next river they reached was a fast-flowing stream, about 150 yards wide and teeming with fish which leaped out of the water. Each of his boys killed about thirty fish with sticks.

A few days later, Dan met another white man, Bainbridge by name, sent out to Africa by the

British Government which was taking over the administration of that part. Bainbridge had had a companion named Kidd who had died, leaving him alone in this lonely outpost. Imagine his amazement when the bearded young Scotsman, wearing slippers because his feet were too sore for boots, appeared out of the unknown bush country. Tins were soon opened and Dan tasted European food once again. Bainbridge insisted on giving Dan clothes and medicines. Dan was most grateful, but would not accept more than a few garments. He was anxious to continue his journey, but Bainbridge persuaded him to stay on for a few days as some mail was expected. It was hardly likely that there would be any for him, but there was, a letter simply addressed:

Dan Crawford,
Central Africa.

It was from his sister and contained a tiny packet of cocoa, just large enough to provide the two white men with a drink.

During the few days the two men were together, Bainbridge opened his heart to Dan, telling him of the loneliness and sadness of his life. Never had he met anyone so happy, so untroubled by the cares of life as this Scottish missionary. Joyfully Dan explained the secret of his happiness—he could never be lonely, for he lived in the company of Jesus. He had no need to worry about things like food and clothes because he was God's servant and God looked after him.

After a few days they separated. Within a week

Bainbridge was dead and Dan was very ill with
malaria. His boys carried him to a place whose
chief was called Mpweto, a young and friendly
man who had heard of the missionary and
gladly welcomed him, giving him yet another
small boy, whom Dan received as one entrusted
to him by God, praying that he would become a
future Christian leader. He recovered his health
and explored the lake till he came to a point
where the waters found an outlet through the
mountains in a rushing torrent which becomes
the River Congo, one of the greatest rivers in the
world.

Dan and his party crossed the river in their
canoes and made for the village of Chief
Chipungu. He welcomed them gladly and sent
messengers to all the villages around. Within a
short time great crowds flocked to Chipungu's to
see the white man and to hear his message. And
as the missionary looked around him he became
sure that this was where God wanted him to
settle, to build his home, to set up a centre from
which the Gospel could be carried to the tribes
around. The chiefs assured him that he was
welcome to settle wherever he wished. Accord-
ingly he chose two pieces of land, one on the level
of the lake and one higher up. No time was lost.
The agreement was confirmed by the firing of
two bullets—one by Chipungu and one by Konga
Vantu (Dan Crawford)—into a tree, the marks
of which remained for many years afterwards.

Soon after this Dan again became very ill. For

the second time within a few weeks he prepared himself for death. He knew no fear of death, but he clung hard to life because he longed to spread the Gospel in this needy part of Africa. It was yet another attack of malaria and it developed into blackwater fever, a severe form of the disease. Dan had never felt so weak before. For three days he lay unconscious and his boys were sure that he was dying. They even discussed how they should bury him. But God had much work for him to do yet and gradually he began to recover. When able to get about again, he had lost count of time and was not sure what date to put in his diary.

However, he began his return journey to Lofoi. Back once more over the mountains where one of his companions, carefully climbing down the steep precipice, was so intent on finding a secure foothold that he did not notice that he was being stalked by a lion. Suddenly the lion sprang —towards a narrow ledge, too narrow, in fact, for it to gain a foothold, and it fell to its death many hundreds of feet, with every bone in its body broken.

The welcome he received from the simple folk at Lofoi moved him deeply. Knowing that twice since leaving them he had been very near to death, they came out to meet him, weeping for joy at seeing him again. To his sister Dan was able to write: "If . . . you dare think of me as being alone and friendless, even from an earthly view, banish the thought. I have brave, loyal hearts around me, who have no father in the world (as they *often*, *often* say) but myself." He looked forward to the time when his boys—seven had been added to his family on this journey— would live in neat, little houses and would spend their days in school or at work and, above all, would be learning about the things of God.

x

THE MOVE TO CHIPUNGU'S

DURING the first few months of 1894, Dan was busy translating portions of the Scriptures into the language spoken by the largest number of those among whom he lived. He now had about thirty boys and young men in his "family", most of them former slaves whom he had set free, and one girl, Sombo by name.

In July, 1894, Dan left Lofoi with his band of loyal followers. Once again he made his way towards the range of mountains which lay between there and Lake Mweru, but this time he intended to find a way round them instead of going over them. At the end of the first day's journey they set up their encampment with a camp fire in the centre. Dan, their "father" as they called him, was preparing his bed when he heard a movement in the bush. Next, out of the darkness into the flickering light of the fire, came a fully-armed man. Behind him came another and another, and women, carrying loads upon their heads, and children.

Dan ordered the newcomers to squat down on the ground; then he fed the fire until it glowed brightly and he could see the dozens of faces and ask them why they had come. They were the people of Lofoi and they had come because they wished to stay with Konga Vantu, the "Gatherer of the People". "You are our father," one of them said. "We are your children. Where you go, there we will go. We will not leave you."

Dan saw that these people had made up their minds to go with him. They had left their homes and their crops. They had thrown away the handles of their hoes as a sign that they would not need them again in Lofoi. What could he do but agree to take them? But there must be conditions. He warned them that they would have to give up old ways of life, that they must forget any quarrels they had had among themselves and that they must obey him. All this they solemnly promised to do and then they lay down to sleep for the night. In the morning, when he could count them, he found that his "family" had increased by 130 men and women, as well as a large number of children and babies. They came from no fewer than ten tribes and two of them were Arabs. Truly he had earned his name of "Gatherer of the Peoples".

The journey before them was one of about 150 miles. Dan took it in easy stages, a few miles each day, and hardly a day passed on which they were not joined by others, men and women, weary of the unrest which had followed the death of Mushidi, and hopeful that this young white chief would lead them to a place where they could enjoy peace and prosperity.

Each night they built for themselves a stockade, circular and about forty yards across, and each night around the camp fire Dan taught them to thank the great God who was watching over them and to pray that their needs might be supplied and that they might be safely guided to their new home. They did not need to worry about food. The people of the villages through which they passed readily loaded them with gifts of food.

The faith of these folk in Dan Crawford was really extraordinary. In all the wonderful history of Africa there has never been anything quite like it.

At last, after about a month on the march, there came into view the waters of the lake, stretching as far as the eye could see, just as the sea does at the seaside. "The Great White Water" the Africans call it because of the way it shines so brightly in the sun. For most of them it was a sight such as they had never seen before. The only water they had known was that of a river.

But his difficulties were not yet over by a long way. Not far from Chipungu's, on an island in the lake, Shimba the outlaw had established his headquarters. From this centre his men carried out raids on neighbouring villages. Three times the Belgians attempted to capture Shimba and each time they were beaten off. On the last occasion, the outlaw not only killed many of the Belgian native troops, but found the canoes by which they had crossed to his island and smashed them, so that the survivors could not get back to the mainland. Only the presence with them of local boatmen, able to build strong rafts from the trees around them, saved their lives.

The survivors made their way to Dan Crawford's little town, where the Belgian officer in charge of the expedition said that he wished everyone to leave the area, so that there would be no one for Shimba to attack. Dan, sure that his God had sent him there and would protect him from the outlaws, protested most strongly. After some discussion, the Belgian officer agreed to put the matter to the local chiefs and allow them to stay if they were determined to do so.

Thus it came about that one afternoon, in this remote part of Africa, a very strange scene was enacted. A small platform was put up. The chiefs with their elders gathered to hear what the Belgian had to say. In his splendid uniform and with a gleaming sword at his side, the Belgian captain took his seat on the platform. Dan, in shorts and a patched jacket, sat on a stool below. A crowd of several hundreds watched the scene from behind the chiefs. The Belgian, through an interpreter, made his little speech, explaining to the people that they must either leave the area with him to find a place of safety or stay with the missionary, in which case he could not promise to protect them from the raiders on the island.

Quietly the great crowd listened until he had finished speaking. Then one of their number arose and spoke. Instead of giving a direct answer, he told a story. It went something like this:

Once upon a time there was a little musk-rat (the smallest of African animals). For many days he lived by the bank of a broad river until one day he grew old and died, lying on his back with his four feet sticking straight up in the air.

Next day the women came to the river to fill their water pots and they saw the poor little musk-rat and they told the king. He came with his big drum and his little drum and his musical clappers. His women danced and their anklets jingled. His men danced and his boys danced and they sang:

"Little musk-rat has died right here,
By the side of the river has musk-rat died.
And the name of the river it shall be this—
'Where the little musk-rat died' river."

After that, whenever the women went to get water, they said they were going to "Where the little musk-rat died" river.

Now one day, there came to that land a great big, roaring elephant and he heard the women singing their song. It made him very angry that

a great river should be called after so tiny and
unimportant a creature as a musk-rat. He decided
that he would alter all that. So he tore up the
trees and he flattened the grass around by
stamping on it. Then he lay down on his back,
stuck his four legs in the air and died, saying to
himself as he drew his last breath, "Now they'll
change the name to the 'Where the great
elephant died' river."

Next day the women came to the river to fill
their water pots and they saw the great elephant
and they told the king. He came with his big
drum and his little drums and his musical
clappers. His women danced and their anklets
jingled. His men danced and his boys danced and
they sang:

"The great big elephant has died right here;
    The great big elephant's dead.
He died on the bank of the big, broad river,
    The 'Where the little musk-rat died' river."

When the speaker had finished his story, he sat
down. The interpreter completed his translation,
but the Belgian officer was most puzzled. Turning
to Dan, he asked him if he knew what the story
meant. Dan, because he had lived in such close
contact with the natives, had understood the
strange story. He was able to tell the official
that the people wanted to stay. The interpreter
agreed that this was the correct interpretation,
but the Belgian officer was not satisfied. He said
he must have a straightforward answer. The
chiefs, seeing that he was too stupid to understand

their little parable, then said that they intended to stay with their beloved friend and leader, Konga Vantu.

You see, the musk-rat represented the missionary who had come first and had shown himself their friend. The elephant represented all the powers of officialdom which had come along afterwards.

Not long after this, the Belgians marched away from the district and the chiefs brought their people to Dan's town from all the villages around. He built a strong fence around the fast-growing community. He could not rely on guns to keep his people safe from raiding outlaws, for he had used his last cartridge many months before. What, therefore, did he do? The answer I will give you in the words of Mushimishi, formerly one of Mushidi's executioners but now Dan's most loyal follower: "Do what he always did; shut the gate at sundown and trust his great God."

But Shimba and his band of outlaws were nearing the end of their reign of terror. Not many months after this, Shimba's gun became caught in his clothing. Somehow or other the trigger was jerked and the outlaw fell dead. His second in command was a man named Senami. Dan went over to the island to make contact with him. He sent a messenger ahead to ask for a meeting without guns. But the messenger was chased back by as ugly looking a mob of scoundrels as ever Dan had seen. Every one of them was wearing a necklace made from human teeth from those he had killed, and some of these necklaces were so long that they hung nearly to the waist.

Dan showed no fear. He kept calm and he put his trust in God. He smiled cheerfully in answer to their bloodcurdling yells. Having no one to quarrel with, the scoundrels eventually quietened down. "In the evening," Dan wrote, "over the faggots, God shut the mouths of the wild beasts and they crowded round to listen. One after another rough fellow blurted out his desire to have done for ever with murder and loot."

Many years later, Dan received a visit from Prince Albert, who became King Albert of the Belgians. He told his royal visitor the story of the musk-rat and the elephant. The Prince asked him to explain the meaning of the story. He told him what you already know, that it meant that the work of the Christian missionaries would outlast all the efforts of government officials. And Dan, as a faithful servant of God, reminded the earthly king of the claims of his Master, the King of kings, who would one day reign supreme.

XI

NO LONGER ALONE

DAN CRAWFORD had been in Africa over four years. Sometimes he had had a white companion, but for most of the time he had been on his own living among the natives, and with no one to whom he could speak in his own language and no one who shared his love for the Lord Jesus Christ.

Soon after his arrival at Chipungu, events began to happen which ensured that he would never again know the loneliness of being the only follower of Christ in a vast area of heathenism. To begin with, another missionary arrived, Mr. Campbell by name. He had followed the same route as Dan and it had taken him two years.

Hardly had the new missionary had time to settle down than news reached them that Mr. Arnot was on his way to Chipungu and was bringing with him another missionary, an Irishman, named Benjamin Cobbe.

You may remember that it was Mr. Arnot who had first explored that particular region, who had met Mushidi and obtained a promise from him that missionaries should be allowed to settle in his capital. Arnot had intended that the main centre of mission work should be near Mushidi's capital. He was not at first pleased to hear that this young Scottish worker had decided to establish the headquarters elsewhere.

He and Cobbe approached Chipungu from the east, having been helped on their way by a trading company, the African Lakes Corporation. So quick was this route that they took only four months from England to the shores of Lake Mweru.

Dan went to meet them and conducted them to his little town. He did not say much about it, so that when Arnot climbed the cliff and suddenly saw in front of him the rows of neat, well-kept huts, dominated by a large church, he had the surprise of his life. At once he was overjoyed at what the Lord had done and there was certainly no word of complaint about the removal from Mushidi's.

When Dan heard how quickly and easily Arnot and Cobbe had reached Lake Mweru, an idea came to him which had lain at the back of his mind for six years. Do you remember reading that when Dan and the other missionaries were travelling round England they met in Bath a gentleman named Tilsley? He was by profession a chemist and dentist, but his chief interests were in God's work. As each of his children was born, he undertook to pay for the cost of keeping a child in George Müller's Homes at Bristol. Having nine children of his own, he thus paid for the upkeep of nine orphans as well.

One of the nine children was a young lady of

about Dan's age, Grace Tilsley. He had felt
drawn to her when he visited their home six years
earlier. In Africa he had given up all thought of
marriage, but the news of a comparatively quick
route from England to Lake Mweru encouraged
him to think that after all it might be possible for
a brave women to undertake the journey. He
prayed much about what he should do next. He
knew that women missionaries would be needed
there and in the end he felt that God was leading
him to write to Miss Tilsley (he did not even
know her Christian name) and invite her to
share his life among these folk in the heart of
Africa.

For all Dan knew, Grace Tilsley might have
married during the six years that had passed
since he had seen her. There was no organized
postal service across Africa in those days and his
letter took a long time to reach her. Thus he had
to wait many months for an answer, so long in
fact that he had given up all hope of ever
receiving one.

Meanwhile, Grace Tilsley had felt that God
was calling her to serve Him as a missionary in
Africa and with that future in view had trained
as a nurse.

Can you imagine her astonishment when she
received a proposal of marriage from someone
she hardly knew? In those days it was most
unusual for a woman to go alone on even a short
journey and this meant travelling thousands of
miles and facing many dangers. As she sought

guidance from God, she became sure that it was
His will that she should accept Dan's proposal.
She, therefore, wrote to him, saying that she
would marry him at a place called Blantyre. This
was the nearest place to Lake Mweru where they
could be married, it being necessary to have a
British consul to perform the ceremony. She did
not have to travel to Africa alone. Three other
missionaries were going out to join Dan and she
was able to go with them. So long did her letter
take to reach Dan and so quickly did she travel
that she was in Blantyre before Dan received the
letter. Now imagine his surprise, after making up
his mind that she was not even going to reply,
to learn that she was already in Africa waiting
for him. You can be sure that he lost no time in
getting there. The newly-married couple spent
their honeymoon travelling from Blantyre back
to Luanza, as Dan's new town was called. Mrs.
Crawford was the first white woman to travel in
that part of the country.

During the months when he had been waiting
for a reply to his letter, something else had
happened that brought great joy to Dan and
ensured that he would never again lack the
company of others who loved the Lord Jesus.
This most memorable event was the first African
convert—and that convert was none other than
Mushimishi.

As a youth, he had become one of Mushidi's
executioners. Many a time he had slaughtered
those who had offended his royal master, with

as little feeling as a butcher kills pigs or sheep to provide us with our Sunday dinner. One day, however, he had to execute a young woman, the mother of a small baby. As he held over her head the stone with which he was going to smash her skull, she pleaded with him to be kind to her baby. Her plea and the cry of the baby as its mother was killed disturbed his conscience which had become hardened to the sight of murder and cruelty.

When Dan Crawford came to the court of Mushidi, preaching the Gospel of Jesus Christ, who taught His followers to love one another, Mushimishi heard the message. When Dan left to go to Lofoi, it was Mushimishi who directed him just as he was taking a wrong path into the bush which would have added many weary miles to his journey. Dan then took the opportunity of telling the African of the two paths through life, only one of which leads to Heaven and to God.

Mushimishi was not prepared then to become a Christian, but he took the first step. He left Mushidi's and went with Dan. He had been with him ever since, travelling from village to village and helping to build the new town on the bluff above the lake.

When Arnot was leaving Dan after his short visit, the two men prayed and sang hymns together. Then, quite unexpectedly, Mushimishi rose and said that he wished to speak. "The God-words," he said, "have reached my heart; now they are coming out of my mouth." He went on to tell them about the poor woman and her baby and other incidents which had led him to Christ. "Why should I not speak?" he asked. "For over against my many sins stands the Atonement made by Jesus for us black people as well as you white folk!"

You can imagine the great joy which the conversion of the former executioner brought to Dan and to Mr. Arnot. By Christmas, 1895, after five years of witness, there were six Christians in Luanza—three missionaries, two Africans from the west converted through Mr. Arnot and Mushimishi. It was little enough to show for all that had been done and suffered, but at least it was a beginning.

XII

LUANZA

THE site which Dan had chosen for his village soon proved too small for all the people who wished to live there. He, therefore, set about looking for a larger site. Eventually he found an ideal place close by a river called the Luanza. It was healthy and there was plenty of room for laying out gardens and the growing of crops.

Mr. Arnot had brought him many useful things, including a good gun and a supply of seeds. The months after Arnot's departure were busily occupied in laying out the new town, building houses and planting seeds. Dan insisted that each house should have two or three rooms, that each compound should be fenced around to give the family living there a little privacy, and that there should be good drains and sanitation, things that Africans had never before thought necessary. It was their habit when their villages became too filthy to live in to move on and build fresh houses elsewhere. But filth breeds disease and Dan was teaching them that they could not hope to be healthy unless they were clean.

As soon as the building work was well under way, Dan set off again to visit the villages, gossiping the Gospel, that is, telling to all who would listen the ages old story of God's love for sinners. With him went the faithful Mushimishi. When he arrived back in Luanza, he found to his joy that the largest house in the town—the "House of God"—was finished.

Soon afterwards Dan set out for Lake Nyasa to meet the three missionaries whom he had heard were coming. It was on the way there that he heard that they had already arrived and that with them was the future Mrs. Dan Crawford.

More than once Dan had seen a missionary get married and then give up his work. He was determined that it would not be so in his case. He had said that "a missionary married was a missionary marred" (spoiled). The Crawfords showed that marriage was anything but a hindrance. Mrs. Crawford possessed qualities which Dan lacked. For example, if the roof leaked Dan would probably not have noticed. If he did notice he would probably have done nothing about it. But his wife not only noticed it; she insisted that it should be repaired at once. She put grass mats on the floor to keep down the dust. With her sewing machine—the first ever seen there—she made cloth ceilings to keep the dust from falling on to everything. She mended clothes as soon as they needed mending. She insisted that meals were eaten at regular times. She took over the care of the garden and made it the best for miles around.

Fever remained one of their chief enemies. It was not long before Mrs. Crawford became ill, but she recovered fairly quickly. Some areas of the country were so dangerous to enter because of the fever that Dan felt a special challenge to faith. Those who lived in the fever-ridden parts needed Christ as much as those who lived in healthier places.

The newly-arrived missionaries had brought with them, in pieces, a large boat for use on the lake. It had been paid for by Christian people in Gourock, who were proud of the great things that Dan had done in Africa since he left them.

XIII

VISIT TO ILALA

IT is not possible to write about Central Africa without mention of David Livingstone. Like Dan Crawford he was a Scotsman. He spent the greater part of his life exploring Africa and in doing so became widely known and greatly loved by the many tribes he visited. When he died in 1873, devoted African followers cut out his heart and buried it. Then they carried his body to the coast, a remarkable journey, often among hostile peoples. The body was then taken on to a British ship, carried to England and laid among the most famous of our race in Westminster Abbey.

In his footsteps followed other missionaries and explorers, among them Fred Arnot and Dan Crawford. It had long been on Dan's mind to visit Ilala, the place where Livingstone had died, and where his heart had been buried. In the summer of 1897 came the opportunity to do so and he set out with his wife and a party of Africans.

After a few weeks, Dan came to places where he had not been before. He boldly denounced the cruel customs of heathenism which he saw being practised. In one place he found that babies who cut the upper teeth first or could not walk at a certain age were cruelly murdered. When a chief died, his old nurse or one of his wives would be killed and buried with him, so that he would not enter the next world alone.

In one place the Crawfords found all the men and boys working in iron. Their tools and methods were primitive compared with modern ironworkers, but, even so, they turned out large quantities of weapons and farming implements.

As Dan pressed on towards Ilala, he was saddened that in this part of Africa, where Livingstone had spent the last days of his earthly life, there were as yet no followers of Christ. One chief gave Dan four oxen and three goats and said he was willing for a missionary to live among his people; but it was because he expected to gain importance for himself by having a white man at his court, rather than because he wanted to gain a knowledge of God.

On July 31st, 1897, the Crawfords reached the tree, almost unvisited by white folk in the twenty-four years since Livingstone had died. Noting that it was a fruit tree, they prayed that before long the fruits of Livingstone's travels would be seen in a turning to Christ in that part of Africa and the end of those things against which Livingstone had fought so brave a fight— slavery, cruelty and superstition.

Close by was the grave of Chitambo, a chief who had shown great kindness to Livingstone.

The Crawfords camped nearby and found a firestone which the great missionary-explorer had used to steady his cooking pots.

They cleared away the bush around the tree and put up a fence to protect it. On a tree nearby Dan carved their initials and the date.

The year of 1898 was a memorable one in the history of Luanza. It began with the death of one of the missionaries, Mr. Gammon, but death to a Christian is not a thing to be feared or grieved over. To Mr. Gammon it was like reaching harbour after a stormy voyage. When he knew that only a few hours of life were left to him, he said calmly, "I'll sail in the morning . . . When I go set the clock going at 'Home Sweet Home' " (this referred to a clock belonging to Mrs. Crawford which played that tune).

Next they received the news that a large party of missionaries was leaving England to join them. In October, a son was born to the Crawfords and by the end of the year there were no fewer than ten missionaries there, four of them women.

In 1899 Dan undertook the last of his exploring journeys, the main object of which was to find the most suitable places for setting up mission stations. Life was rarely dull. One day he found himself surrounded—with a hundred poisoned arrows pointing at him; another time his little craft was attacked by an angry hippopotamus. Dan held his fire until the beast was only five yards away, then fired at its throat, killing it almost instantly. One day he saw a boy taken by a crocodile before he could do anything to save the lad. He met another boy whose life had been saved because he had a toe missing on his left foot. He was to have been offered as a human sacrifice at a funeral, but was spared because the natives would not offer an imperfect body as a sacrifice to their gods.

On this journey, he met Dr. Laws, another famous missionary, who promised to help Dan with the printing of his translation of the New Testament.

When he arrived back at Luanza, he learned that one of the missionaries, John Wilson, had died—and also his own baby son, just a week after his first birthday.

A second son was born to the Crawfords in July, 1900. They lived together for a few months after this and then Mrs. Crawford returned to Britain with her baby. She left him in the care of Dan's mother, while she returned to Luanza. It was a great sacrifice for both of them to make, but they made it for the sake of Him who had given His own Son for them.

XIV

THE LANGUAGE PROBLEM

I EXPECT some of you have often wished that everyone on earth could speak the same language. You probably do not find it easy to learn another language unless you are one of those rare people who have a gift for learning languages. Dan Crawford had this gift.

He was able to speak about a dozen tongues. He learned not only the African languages in which he preached the Gospel and into which he translated the Scriptures; he learned Greek and Hebrew, the tongues in which the Bible was first written. He was then able to translate direct from the original languages into the various African dialects. Moreover, he spoke Portuguese and French so well that the officials with whom he had to deal were amazed,

He translated the Scriptures and he wrote nearly 400 hymns in the languages of Central Africa. During his first few years in Africa, he carried note books with him wherever he went. In these he jotted down notes about new words and idioms. By living closely to the people and for a long time without contact with white men, he learned to think as an African. He was able to understand Africans and their ways when government officials and others were unable to do so. We had an example of this in the story of the little musk-rat.

When tropical storms made travel impossible, Dan would stay in his hut translating. It was work that he loved to be doing, for he loved the Book and longed for the day when the Africans around him could read it for themselves. He knew that within its pages they would find the Saviour.

He paid special attention to African sayings and proverbs. I told you in an earlier chapter how his being able to quote a proverb about a ferryman resulted in Dan getting compensation for goods that had been lost. Often, when preaching the Gospel, he was able to turn an African saying to his own end. They had a proverb, "To the blind there is no day dawn." To this Dan answered, "Since the days of Bartimaeus there has been" (Bartimaeus was the blind man to whom Jesus gave sight; *Mark* 10:46-52).

Again, the African farmer says of the seed, "It went away naked into the cold dark loam; but when it came again it came richly dressed." Dan could then quote the words of our Lord, "Except a corn of wheat fall into the ground and die, it abideth alone" (*John* 12:24).

Not many people have translated the whole of the Bible; but Dan Crawford did so—into the Luba language. So well did he perform this task that educated Africans, themselves able to compare his translation with other versions of the Scriptures have paid it the compliment of saying that it is in their own language and not in "the white man's dialect."

So closely did Dan study the Scriptures as he worked on the translations that he said it seemed as if he had never really known his Bible before. Sometimes he found that the original could be more easily translated into Luba than into English.

When his translation was ready for printing, he took his precious manuscript to Nyasaland where Dr. Laws had a printing press. The National Bible Society of Scotland paid for and published Dan's New Testament. At first few copies could be used, for not many of the people could read.

Great was Dan's joy when the first New Testaments arrived from the printers. There were tears of joy, followed by songs of praise, and prayers that God would bless His Word. These Testaments were the first books ever printed in the Luba language. There were no newspapers to record the event, but the news quickly spread and those who had learned to read sat up all night reading.

The translation of the whole Bible took much longer. In fact Dan did not finish it until a few months before his death and did not live to see it in print.

He did, however, see the results of sending out the Testaments. His faith in the power of the

Book was justified again and again. One example which shows us how wonderfully God's Word can lead men to know the Lord Jesus followed the giving by Dan of one of his New Testaments to a Roman Catholic priest. The priest gave it to a criminal condemned to death, whom he was visiting in prison, and the criminal, in reading it, found Christ as his Saviour. Thus does God use His Word and bless those who read it.

In Nyasaland, at the mission centre founded by Dr. Laws, Dan saw that those who had learned to read went back to their villages able to read the New Testament to their people. In this way many more were hearing the Gospel than could be reached by European missionaries.

What was also of great importance, the spread of the Bible did much to answer the errors of other religions—the Arabs who held that Mohammed was greater than Christ and the Roman Catholics who worshipped our Lord's mother and prayed to her.

Christian missionaries, by placing their book in the hands of Africans, had an advantage over the Arabs who regarded their book, the Koran, as too sacred to place in the hands of unbelievers.

Towards the end of 1900, an epidemic of smallpox, spreading through the region, reached Luanza. This is the disease against which you are vaccinated. Mrs. Crawford had some vaccine, but it proved of little use, for it did not "take" except in a few cases.

The disease spread among the people at

Luanza and many died, among them Mrs. Higgins, a coloured missionary from the West Indies, and Mushimishi, the first convert, who became the first African in that part to die in the Christian faith. His death made a deep impression, for it was quite unlike the deaths with which Africans were familiar. Mushimishi had put his trust in the Lord Jesus and he passed away peacefully, whispering his Saviour's name and urging his friends and relatives to forsake their old gods and follow Christ. Nor did he plead with them in vain. One of his old friends, Kapenda by name, gave up his heathen ways and became the second convert. And a true Christian he proved to be, witnessing boldly for Christ for many years.

More conversions followed. A young man named Mirambo declared himself "a Christ's man." A married couple came to Dan in the evenings to receive instruction as they desired to be Christians. A youngster named Chungu declared, "I now know that God's call is to repent and believe the good news; and that Christ is He who brings us into reconciliation with God; and that the believer has unending life." Then there was a man named Kalala, described by Dan as "the oldest and hardest sinner in Luanza." He became very ill and, lying at the gate of death, found peace in believing in the Lord Jesus.

After all the years of sowing, Dan was beginning to see the harvest. There were many more besides those I have mentioned. Most of them were men and boys. Whenever converts were baptized, huge crowds gathered to witness the sight of Africans boldly taking their stand as Christians.

By 1905, when Dan had been more than fifteen years in Africa, he could speak of a church of African Christians. In November of that year, eight Africans were baptized on one occasion. He was always very careful to make sure that those who professed to have become Christians had been really converted. He knew that in some lands, when the Gospel had been first preached, men and women had professed faith in hopes of personal gain. "Rice Christians" he called them, that is, those who called themselves Christians for the rice or other food they would receive. Our Lord would not allow His followers to make him a king by force. Nor does He force any of us to make Him King of our lives. He wants us to accept Him as our Saviour and own Him willingly as our King.

xv

DAN GOES ROUND THE WORLD

EARLY in the year 1911, Dan was troubled by a threat on the part of the Belgian authorities to remove everyone who lived in the vicinity of Lake Mweru. The reason for this threat was the supposed danger of sleeping sickness, one of the terrible diseases which every year was killing many thousands in Africa.

Dan knew that the site which he had chosen for his town was healthy, and this fact was eventually realized by the Belgians. In order to persuade the officials to allow the people of Luanza to remain undisturbed, Dan set out for the town from which the area was governed. This was a new town, springing up not far from Mushidi's old capital. In 1910 the Belgians had ordered that the town was to be built. It was to be called Elisabethville, after the Queen of the Belgians (see if you can find it on a map of Africa). Today it is a pretty town, some of the streets of which are cobbled, and is surrounded by pleasant grassy meadows. The houses are picturesque and windows and doors are painted bright red. But when Dan came to it in 1911 the buildings were just springing up where none had stood before.

While on the way there, he heard that the authorities had changed their minds. His people at Luanza would be allowed to remain. However, he had gone too far to turn back and he decided to go on and use the opportunity for dealing with other matters.

Arriving in Elisabethville, he saw for the first time in over twenty years a railway train and for the first time in his life a motor car, for the petrol engine had been perfected during the years that Dan had been living in the heart of the African forests.

With Bible in hand and alert as usual for the opportunity to spread the Good News, Dan walked through the streets of the growing city. He saw there many natives who knew him and were able to sing hymns which he had written and taught them. A British funeral gave him an opportunity to make known God's offer of salvation. There being no minister, Dan led the funeral procession. With Bible open he preached the Gospel at the graveside—"an offer of life by the grave of death" he called it.

The Governor of the Congo, a Belgian general who had stayed at Luanza with the Crawfords, invited Dan to be his guest. While staying at the Governor's house, Dan received a cheque for £100 from a gentleman whom he did not know. He had been thinking of making a visit to Britain and this gift came to him as a sign from God, for it provided him with the means for the journey. The Governor, who was about to visit Lake Mweru, promised to escort Mrs. Crawford to Elisabethville and in May, 1911, they began their long journey. Reaching civilization at Johannesburg, they travelled south to Cape Town, from where they came to England by sea.

They landed at Southampton and naturally the first place to which Dan wanted to go was Scotland to see once again the mother from whom he had been separated for twenty-two years and his son whom he had only seen as a tiny baby.

Those who met Dan during his first few weeks

in Britain noticed that he walked very strangely, lifting his feet unusually high as though he was stepping over obstacles. It was, of course, a habit he had acquired through much trekking in bush country.

No sooner was he back than he began to receive invitations to speak about his work in Africa. He travelled up and down the country, telling Christian people of the wonderful way in which God had used him. In between the meetings, he spent much of his time writing a book. "Thinking Black" he called it, a reference to the way he had always tried to see things from the black man's point of view.

Whether in Africa or England or Scotland, Dan was still a missionary. Every day he tried to speak to at least one person about the Lord Jesus. He preached the Gospel on Epsom Downs to the racegoers at the Derby. When travelling by train, he spoke to his fellow passengers about the claims of Christ.

One day he was travelling to Scotland by train and in the railway carriage had the joy of leading a young man to Christ. He gave the young convert his address, which was that of his publishers. A few days later he was in their office in London when a letter was handed to him from a nurse who had heard him speak the previous week-end in Scotland. She had felt that God wanted her to give him £4 which she had set aside as a gift for His work, but she had not seen Dan after the meeting and did not know his address. However, on the morning after the meeting she had gone to nurse an elderly lady, whom she found over-joyed because her son had been led to Christ through a conversation with someone whom he had met on the train. It was, indeed, the same Dan Crawford to whom she wished to send her gift. Moreover, it was exactly the sum he needed to cover his week-end expenses. In ways such as these did Dan often prove that God knew his needs and never failed to provide for him.

From England Dan crossed to America, where another incident occurred which showed how God rewarded this simple faith. He had changed his suit and had gone out, completely forgetting to take any money with him. He had not had to show a ticket before boarding his train. He had no papers with him to prove his identity. He was on the train, speeding from one American city to another, when he suddenly realized what he had done. The question was, what should he do next? Well, he first told his Father (God) what had happened; then he looked around his fellow passengers, finally deciding to sit opposite one of them, tell him who he was and ask for a loan of money. The gentleman thus approached gazed in amazement at Dan. Then he turned his news-paper round and showed the missionary a picture of himself. It turned out that the gentleman whom Dan had approached was deeply interested in the work of Christian missions. The result of that strange meeting was that Dan not only received the loan he needed, but in the years that followed he received large sums of money for his work in Luanza.

One American newspaper interviewed Dan and wrote a lengthy account of his answers to their questions. Knowing that he would be returning to Africa soon afterwards, they asked him if he would ever leave it again. "I cannot tell you," he answered, "how much work there is to be done at home and I am going home to do it." Notice how Dan used the word "home". Africa, to which God had called him, was his home, not Scotland, the land of his birth and boyhood. While so much remained to be done in Africa, he could not spare much time for visiting other lands.

From America he went on to Australia and while he was there the Great War of 1914-18 began. He was soon to be found preaching to young men who were about to go overseas to the battlefields of Europe. His message was the same as that which he preached in the heart of the Congo, that Jesus Christ came into the world to save sinners.

Early in 1915, Dan was at sea again, on his way to South Africa. When he landed there he had sailed right round the world. He now came up against the "colour bar", laws and customs which in some countries separate people because of the colour of their skins. It grieved Dan to see his black friends compelled to worship God in separate churches and to travel in separate railway compartments. He knew that in God's sight the black men were as precious as white men.

He found himself on one occasion travelling in a third class railway compartment (normally only used by Africans) when he received an invitation to sit with a general who was travelling first class. Dan replied that as his ticket would not allow him to go into the first class compartment, the general must come to him. This the general did, for he was eager to meet the famous missionary and as the train rattled northwards, taking Dan nearer and ever nearer to his beloved people at Luanza, the two men knelt together and the general placed his life under the command of the Lord Jesus Christ.

XVI

BUILDING A STRONG CHURCH

WE can try to imagine the joy with which Konga Vantu was welcomed back to Luanza after an absence of four years. He warned the people of his approach by firing a rifle. Then they came rushing out to meet him, yelling for joy. It was a day which Dan would never forget, but so moving was the experience that he could not find words to describe it.

Twenty-five years had gone by since Dan had first entered the kingdom of Mushidi to begin his great work of evangelization. He marvelled

at what God had done and at the great changes
which had taken place. No longer did he feel that
he must ever be pushing out to new areas. The
African Christians were the ones best able to
evangelize their fellow Africans. His task was to
build up a strong Christian church, from which
native evangelists would carry the Gospel to
every village and dwelling, until all should know
of Jesus the Saviour.

There were by now Roman Catholic missionaries in the Katanga. In their schools they were
teaching the Africans that they should pray to
our Lord's mother and should wear small crosses
round their necks. Such ornaments were not very
different from the fetishes which they had worn
in connection with their heathen beliefs. Converts
to the Christian faith would promptly burn their
fetishes. It seemed to Dan that to encourage them
to wear other ornaments might lead to the
ornament becoming more important than the
unseen Lord. His answer to these and other
errors was to spread the Scriptures. He still had
much to do to translate the whole Bible into the
Luba tongue. His slogan was "A Bible in every
hut in the land."

As he grew older he became less able to undertake long and dangerous journeys, but he never
lost any of his love for the peoples of Africa. He
spoke of the Lord Jesus to young and old and
tried to lead them to Him.

One day he had to ask an African the way.
Proudly the native replied, "Want to know the

way? I am the way." As he spoke he pointed to his chest. Within him lay the knowledge and that was why he could call himself the way. To Dan it was a golden opportunity to tell of One who had used those very words, "I am the Way" (*John* 14:6).

If you think that the Crawfords, engaged in the serious task of winning souls, were unable to get any fun out of life you would be very wrong. They often laughed merrily, for Dan had a grand sense of humour. Once, as they were walking along, they met two fishermen, carrying a load of newly-caught fish. "How many?" called Dan. "A hundred," replied one of the men. Dan's great knowledge of languages caused him to remark that the Swahili word for "hundred" which had been used—"mia" (pronounced mee-ah)—was almost exactly the same as the word which our Lord and Moses and even Abraham had used for the number. He was solemnly pointing out how closely related are the various languages of the human race, when Mrs. Crawford interrupted by saying, "Yes and my old cat Tommie also says mee-ah!"

Again, we hear of Dan keeping the African porters in fits of laughter with his merry jokes. Yes, he who spoke to them earnestly about the most serious things of life could also enjoy a good joke with them. Sometimes he would rise late in the morning before a journey which should have been started early. The impatient Africans might then hear Dan's voice from within his tent imitating their grumbles. Soon their complaints would turn to smiles and the smiles to joyous laughter. By the time Dan emerged from his tent, good humour would have been restored.

In Dan's last few years he was joined at Luanza by his nephew, Dr. G. E. Tilsley, who collected all the material he could about his uncle's wonderful life. Later on he wrote Dan's life story.

Dr. Tilsley gives us a most interesting description of life at Luanza at the time of his arrival in the early 1920's. There were about 400 houses there, each of which had several rooms and its own fenced-in courtyard. Five broad, tree-lined streets led to a square in the centre of the town, and here was the church, easily the largest building in Luanza, open to the sky and with seating for about 1,000 people.

In the fields around were crops of manioc, maize, beans, ground nuts, potatoes and rice, with vegetables such as tomatoes, pumpkins and marrows. Then there were fruit trees and flowers. Not in all the Belgian Congo, which is more than ten times the size of Britain, was there a native town to compare with Luanza for beauty and cleanliness.

Dan's own house was built in the same style as the native huts—from local trees, bamboo, bark-rope and mud, with grass thatch about two feet thick. The walls were colour washed, mainly with colours obtained in the neighbourhood of Luanza—white chalk, charcoal with a vegetable dye for black and soils from the hills for shades of red and yellow. Native mats covered the floors and most of the furniture had been made for Dan by other missionaries. In front of the house, Mrs. Crawford had managed to produce a lawn, a very unusual feature in Africa. Above it grew a very fine fig tree, beneath which Dan desired his remains to be buried when God called him Home.

Each day in Luanza began with a service in the church to which the people were called by the town crier. Then they went about their various tasks—fishing, hunting or farming. Those who were unwell went to the clinic, the children to school. It was a truly happy and well organized community.

By 1926 Dan had finished his translation of the whole Bible. Much remained to be done in the way of preparing the manuscript for printing, but the task at which he had laboured for more than thirty years was complete. For those who could read, the whole Bible would soon be available in the Luba tongue.

Dan's death came suddenly as the result of a simple accident. On the night of May 29th, he knocked the back of his left hand against a shelf, causing a cut. The following morning his hand was sore. Dr. Tilsley had come back to England on leave and there was no other doctor to whom he could show it. A day or two later his arm began to swell and caused him great pain. Mrs. Crawford and his native friends did all they could, but nothing could save his life. The poison which had entered through his hand had spread through his body. On the evening of June 3rd he fell asleep in Jesus, having served his Saviour faithfully and well in that part of the great harvest field to which he had been called.

XVII

LUANZA TODAY

SIXTY-FIVE years have gone by since Dan Crawford landed in Africa and set out for Katanga, the kingdom of Mushidi. Today in Luanza there is a flourishing church, with about 250 members. There are other groups of Christians in at least ten of the villages of that area.

About 2,500 boys and girls in Luanza and the villages around go to schools run by the missionaries who are carrying on the wonderful work which Dan began. His translation of the Bible is their main text book, from which they learn to read.

There are African evangelists who visit the villages for miles around to proclaim the same Gospel message of which Dan was for so long the only preacher. In 1951 they had the joy of seeing some 200 people throw off the shackles of heathenism to follow the Lord Jesus Christ. In that same year 104 persons confessed their faith in public baptism. But there are still many who do not know Him.

The bodies of the people are being cared for as well as their souls. The Luanza hospital can take up to 100 patients. There is a special camp for lepers, dispensaries in three of the villages, and clinics for mothers with young babies.

There are many dangers still to be faced by those who are out there—malaria and other tropical diseases, wild animals such as leopards, hyenas, and snakes, and those who would teach the Africans errors and falsehoods.

But, like a lighthouse sending out a bright beam across a dark ocean, Dan's little Christian town sheds abroad the light of the Gospel amid the tribes still floundering in the darkness of heathenism. It is a worthy memorial to the humble Scottish missionary who, in youth and middle age, sickness and health, poverty and sorrow, always pinned his faith in the great God he served and proved that that same God is able to do exceeding abundantly above all that we ask or think.

THE END